HOW DO THEY HELP?
WORLD WILDLIFE FUND

BY KATIE MARSICO

CHERRY LAKE Publishing

Published in the United States of America by Cherry Lake Publishing
Ann Arbor, Michigan
www.cherrylakepublishing.com

Content Adviser: Rob Fischer, Ph.D., Professor and Director, Master of Nonprofit Organizations, Jack, Joseph, and Morton Mandel School of Applied Social Sciences, Case Western Reserve University
Reading Adviser: Marla Conn MS, Ed., Literacy specialist, Read-Ability, Inc.

Photo Credits: © Jean-Edouard Rosey/Shutterstock, cover, 1, 11;
© Defotoberg I Dreamstime.com - WWF Balloon Photo, 5;
© Jurgen Freund/Nature Picture Library/Corbis, 7; © littleny/Shutterstock, 9;
© Steve Debenport/istock, 13; © goodluz/Shutterstock, 15;
© AR Photo / Alamy Stock Photo, 17; © Matt Gibson/Shutterstock, 19; © Fuse/Thinkstock, 21

LIBRARY OF CONGRESS CATALOGING-IN-PUBLICATION DATA
CIP data has been filed and is available at catalog.loc.gov

Cherry Lake Publishing would like to acknowledge the work of The Partnership for 21st Century Learning. Please visit *www.p21.org* for more information.

Printed in the United States of America
Corporate Graphics
CLFA11

WORLD WILDLIFE FUND

CONTENTS

HOW DO THEY HELP?

COMMITTED TO CONSERVATION

To the people of China, the giant panda is a national treasure. Unfortunately, this peaceful bear is in danger of becoming extinct. Hunting and **habitat** loss have reduced the giant panda population to less than 2,000 animals.

World Wildlife Fund (WWF) is determined to change this

WWF uses different ways to let people know about their mission. This balloon is one of them!

LOOK!

Take a closer look at the WWF logo. (A logo is a symbol used to identify an organization.) Why do you think WWF leaders chose to feature the giant panda?

5

situation. WWF is the world's largest **conservation** organization.

Members of WWF carry out conservation efforts in 130 countries, including the United States and Canada. They work to restore, or bring back, animal populations. WWF also focuses on conserving a variety of freshwater, ocean, and forest habitats. It aims to build a future that balances people's needs with respect for the environment and **biodiversity**.

6

Helping kids understand the importance of the environment is a big part of WWF's job.

WWF works to reduce people's ecological footprint, or impact on the environment. The size of an ecological footprint is based on humans' use of natural resources in a certain area. What activities do you think create a larger ecological footprint?

7

A HISTORY OF HELPING

In 1961, a handful of conservation groups existed across the globe. Yet most lacked a steady supply of money to fund their efforts.

Sixteen of the world's leading conservationists tried to solve this problem by forming WWF. It served as a **nonprofit** fund-raising organization. WWF's founders agreed that it would provide financial support to conservation groups around the globe.

WWF works with many other conservation groups, like the Wildlife Conservation Society at the Bronx Zoo.

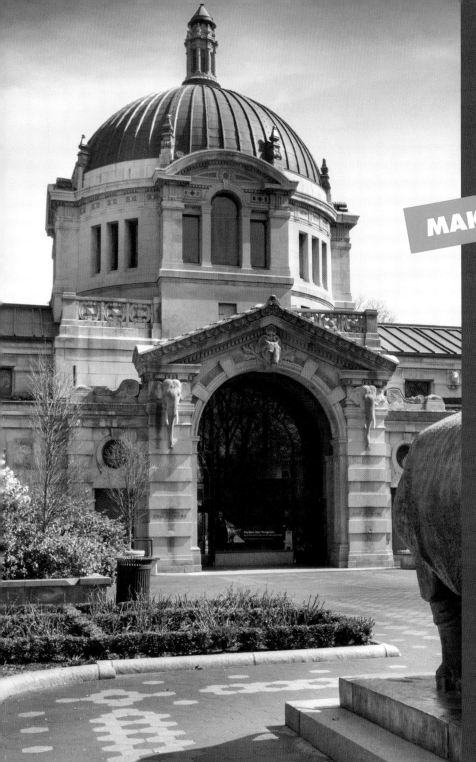

Are you able to guess how much money WWF has spent on conservation projects? Guess big! Since 1961, WWF has provided about $11.5 billion in funding.

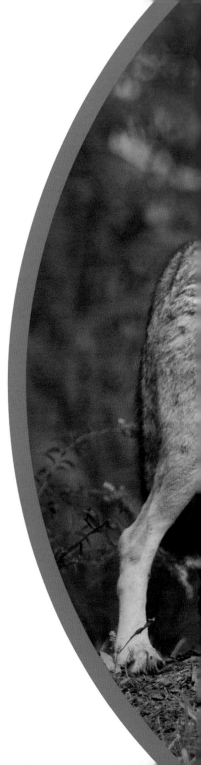

At first, WWF mainly funded projects to protect animals that were being threatened by human activities. The Tule goose in Canada and the red wolf in the United States were two examples of such species. By the early 1970s, however, WWF had broadened its focus. The organization started to set up national parks and nature **reserves**. This allowed WWF to conserve both animals and their natural habitats.

At one time, there were only 14 red wolves left in the world.

Want to find out what other species WWF helps protect? How about which specific habitats it works to conserve? Head online or contact a WWF office to learn more. (U.S. headquarters are in Washington, D.C. Canadian headquarters are in Toronto.)

Today, WWF funds more than 11,000 projects. In addition to partnering with other conservation groups, it **collaborates** with governments, businesses, and local communities. WWF efforts include conserving habitats. They also involve protecting wildlife, finding responsible ways to produce food, and studying how human activities affect Earth's climate.

There are a lot of different ways to practice conservation and sustainable living in your town!

WWF supports programs that promote sustainable living. Such programs encourage people to make choices that use up less of Earth's natural resources. Recycling is one activity that goes hand in hand with sustainable living. Are you able to think of any others?

13

WWF depends on both volunteers and paid employees. Some are scientists who conduct environmental research. Others are educators who create teaching materials that help students learn more about conservation.

Certain WWF workers are lobbyists. They try to influence government officials on issues that impact wildlife and natural habitats. Finally, WWF relies on financial experts and people who work in the media.

Testing water and soil helps scientists learn more about an animal's habitat.

LOOK!

Look for photographs of WWF workers in action! (Hint: The library and Internet are good places to start your search.) What are the people in those pictures doing? How are they supporting conservation?

15

EFFORTS TO SAVE EARTH

WWF uses several methods to support conservation. It builds partnerships with businesses to encourage sustainable living and to save various species and natural settings. Under WWF's guidance, companies learn to develop more environmentally friendly production processes. In turn, these businesses sometimes donate to WWF projects across the globe.

Large businesses can make a big difference in conservation efforts, but individuals can help too!

Are you able to guess how WWF pays for its conservation efforts? (Hint: There's more than one source!) Most of the organization's funding comes from individual contributions. Governments and businesses also provide financial support to WWF.

17

Members of WWF work closely with government officials, as well. They help shape laws that protect wildlife and the environment.

WWF is involved in a great deal of research. Conservationists study **endangered** animals and the condition of natural habitats. In addition, they pay attention to environmental challenges within individual communities. WWF finds ways for residents to be more careful about how they use natural resources.

WWF thinks it is important to conserve the environment for the next generation.

What is WWF doing to save the Amazon rain forest? How is it encouraging cities around the world to conserve energy? Why is WWF concerned about marine turtles? Head online to learn the answers to these and other questions!

19

Finally, WWF believes strongly in the value of public education. It hosts workshops, publishes a magazine, and sponsors television ads. WWF even sells art, clothes, and toys that are designed to teach the importance of conservation.

There's no guarantee that Earth's natural treasures will last forever. Fortunately, WWF is dedicated to helping people learn that lesson before it's too late.

Helping to clean up your community helps WWF reach its goal.

Want to do your part to support WWF? Grab some old magazines, scissors, and glue. Create a collage of images that are related to WWF's conservation efforts. Try to find pictures of wildlife, natural habitats, and people practicing sustainable living!

21

GLOSSARY

biodiversity (bye-oh-duh-VUHR-suh-tee) the existence of many different kinds of plants and animals in a certain environment

collaborates (kuh-LAH-buh-raytes) works with another person or group in order to achieve something

conservation (kan-suhr-VAY-shuhn) the act of protecting the environment and the plants and animals that live in it

endangered (en-DAYN-jurd) at risk of dying out

habitat (HAB-uh-tat) an environment where certain plants and animals are usually found

natural resources (NA-chuh-ruhl REE-sors-uhz) materials or substances such as water and forests that occur in nature and are useful to humans

nonprofit (nahn-PRAH-fit) not existing for the main purpose of earning more money than is spent

reserves (ri-ZURVZ) areas of land or water that are set aside for conservation purposes

FIND OUT MORE

BOOKS

Hawley, Ella. *Exploring Our Impact on the Environment.* New York: PowerKids Press, 2013.

Littlewood, Peter. *Endangered Species.* Mankato, MN: Smart Apple Media, 2012.

Trueit, Trudi Strain. *Giant Pandas.* Mankato, MN: Amicus High Interest/Amicus Ink, 2016.

WEB SITES

National Geographic Kids—Giant Panda
kids.nationalgeographic.com/animals/giant-panda/#giant-panda-eating.jpg
Visit this site for additional information about the endangered animal featured on WWF's logo.

WWF—About Our Earth
wwf.panda.org/about_our_earth/
Head here to learn more about WWF, as well as Earth's many natural treasures!

INDEX

ABOUT THE AUTHOR

Katie Marsico is the author of more than 200 children's books. She lives in a suburb of Chicago, Illinois, with her husband and children.